eeing the Getty Gardens

a Souvenir Book

From the outset, the Getty Center was conceived as a place in which gardens and other outdoor spaces were as integral to its overall character as the architecture. Throughout the planning process, we sought to create an environment in which buildings, gardens, plazas, fountains, and the enveloping hillsides were thoughtfully developed in relationship to the whole and to the surrounding city. At the same time, within a general image of a rustic Mediterranean setting, we deliberately sought to introduce garden and landscape features that were memorable, surprising, dramatic, and even challenging. In the diversity and range of outdoor spaces — and attention to purely aesthetic objectives — the Getty Center is not conventional. We hoped that the landscape and architecture would interact in unexpected ways, embellishing the already dramatic views of city, mountains, and sea and providing moments of quiet and contemplation.

Over the course of several years, we carefully considered the placement, form, and content of the Getty Center's gardens. Architect Richard Meier consulted with internationally respected landscape architects Laurie D. Olin — who, with Meier, designed the basic hilltop plan — and the late Emmett Wemple (designer of the gardens at the Getty Villa in Malibu), who shaped the hillsides and the native environment. We looked to such historic precedents as the Alhambra in Spain and the Villa d'Este in Italy, yet we always remained alert to the reality of late twentieth-century Los Angeles. Not least among our ambitions was to create a worthy addition to the city's public places. To create the Central Garden, we commissioned artist Robert Irwin, asking him to design a provocative and inspiring counterpoint — a garden conceived as an ever-changing work of art.

This book is an attempt to capture the spirit of the Getty Center's gardens and outdoor spaces, to recall their vivid colors and varied textures, and to delight in the lush palette of their plants.

Stephen D. Rountree
Director, Getty Center Building Program, 1984–1997
Executive Vice President and Chief Operating Officer
The J. Paul Getty Trust

Exuberant gardens bring the Getty Center to life, creating oases of beauty amid the formal buildings. The plantings cast interesting shadows, add a fragrance to the scene, dapple light across a facade, or introduce bright red to a palette of beiges. Looking up at the Museum pavilions from under a canopy of native sycamores in the Central Garden, or gazing down at the city as the sunset fades, one can sense the many different aspects of the Getty Center.

The Getty's hilltop site, encircled by chaparral and thousands of oak trees, offers many vistas and experiences. The sunny, arid character of Southern California is reflected in the Getty Center gardens, plazas, fountains, and terraces. Strongly patterned and full of allusions to local as well as historical contexts, this landscape accommodates both ornamental plants such as the bird of paradise — the official flower of Los Angeles — and fruit trees with associations in classical and modern literature.

The changing of the seasons is conspicuously played out in the plantings of the Getty Center grounds and gardens. As jacaranda trees bloom in the summer, as leaves of deciduous sycamores change color and fall, as Boston ivy turns crimson in the autumn and sheds its foliage, the rhythms of nature are accentuated.

The gardens of the Getty Center have many optical surprises. The clouds of purple jacarandas in front of the auditorium are flecked with the flowers of a rare white tree; nearby, a courtyard is planted with kentia palms, tree ferns, philodendron, and crape myrtles. Trees with edible fruit such as figs, lemons, and oranges, strawberry bushes, and vines with grapes grow around the Research Institute. Among the evergreens between pavilions of the Museum is a camphor tree with many trunks; underfoot in the Museum courtyard is aromatic Corsican mint. The desert garden on the south promontory of the Center, a hot and arid zone, is glimpsed unexpectedly. The plants are common enough in Southern California, but the composition of cactus, aloe, and succulents is startling in its graphic design.

The landscape design of the Getty Center marries well with Richard Meier's architecture, adding color to the travertine surfaces, bringing warmth to the geometry, framing portals and passageways that themselves define views of gardens beyond. "We were very sympathetic to the built structures," says landscape architect Laurie D. Olin, "and we gave a great deal of thought to deciding when to leave a wall proud and when to play it up." Rough-hewn travertine slabs serve as seats and relate both to the architecture and to the landscaping.

Whether the eye fixes at close range on a single fern or flower or takes in from a distance a mass of plants and their abstract forms and patterns, perspective plays an important part in the gardens of the Getty Center. Open spaces add scale and visual relief. These compositions are shaped with flora from Asia, South Africa, Mexico, Australia, Europe, and across the United States—and with indigenous plants.

Five water gardens enliven the landscape of the Getty Center with sound and movement. Welcoming visitors to the arrival plaza is a fountain whose water jets rise to meet blue-tinged sprays of plumbago, rosemary, and ceanothus. This shallow pool is fed by a gentle cascade that runs down steps alongside the grand stairway leading to the Museum. On a terrace outside the Museum, water flows through a runnel into a basin and descends and drips down the chiseled walls of a travertine grotto. It seems to reappear as a spring in the upper Central Garden, then rushes downhill to the azalea pool. The Museum courtyard is ornamented by a long basin with forty-six vaulting jets and a secluded pool with rocks and fountain. The large circular pool and fountain—the focal point of the courtyard—combines the sculptural interest of massive, blue-veined marble boulders transported from the Gold Country of Northern California, the playful splashing of water from several sources, and the calm of a reflecting pool. Travertine stepping stones cross the outer pool, while the sound of the adjacent fountain brings a sensation of coolness to the courtyard on even the hottest days.

he Central Garden, designed by Robert Irwin, is a work of art in its own right. Commissioned by the Getty Trust, Irwin's landmark project changes the once-steeper canyon between the Museum and the Research Institute into a highly cultivated sculptural environment, contrasting in form with the buildings looming above. The Central Garden is a study in seasonal transformations, celebrating nature's evanescence.

Robert Irwin, a native of Southern California, began his career as an abstract expressionist painter and later gained renown as a leader of the West Coast Light and Space movement, creating site-specific installations inspired by the vagaries of particular settings. He has spoken of the Central Garden as "a sculpture in the form of a garden aspiring to be art" and observes that the work will always be in the process of becoming. "It's going to take three, seven years for the trees to grow in, the underbrush to fill out," Irwin has said. "That's part of what the garden's about. If you're going to experience it in all its qualities, you have to keep coming back. A garden is a commitment."

Visitors descend into the Central Garden along a zigzagging walkway of sandstone edged in Cor-Ten steel and bordered by London plane trees; their branches are woven together to grow a green canopy over the path. Underfoot, coursing down a rocky bed flanked by Montana Kinesaw stone, a stream is interrupted by waterfalls of carnelian granite from South Dakota. The stream, whose sound is different at each crossing of the path, finally plunges down a stepped stone wall, or "chadar," of the kind seen in Mogul gardens in India. The water ends by becoming a mirror on which seems to float a maze of red, purple, and pink azaleas.

Parasols of bent industrial-steel bars with fuchsia bougainvillea flowing over them speak of the inven
tiveness and whimsy Robert Irwin has brought to the Central Garden. "Irwin believes that each of
us can find something new in ourselves here, if we'll slow down and open ourselves to sensation,"
says John Walsh, director of the Getty Museum. "His work is changing and growing, which art rarely
does! Like all successful works of art, it gives us new surprises each time." The most ambitious of
the Getty gardens and a high point of any visit to the Center, the Central Garden intertwines art and
life in a bold new form.

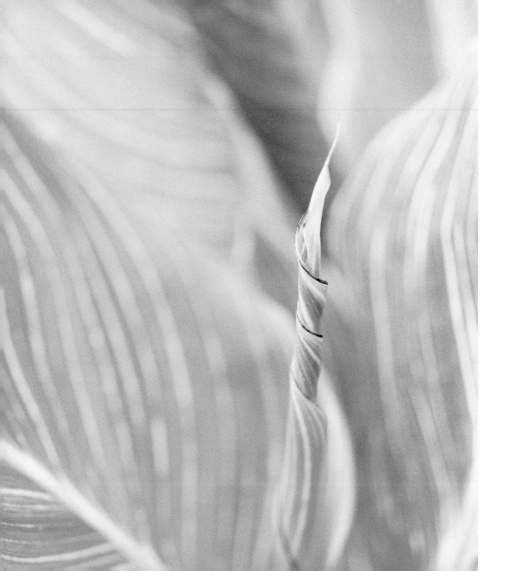

Only one-quarter of the Getty Center is taken up by buildings; the rest of the land is given over to the plantings of an urban park. Earth, water, stone, and wood are some of the elements of these gardens. An astonishing array of plants, flowers, vines, shrubs, grasses, and trees have been introduced into the landscape. A visit to the Center provides a heightened view of nature, literally and figuratively; it is an occasion to ramble and rest, to let the imagination run free, and to rediscover the realm of the senses.

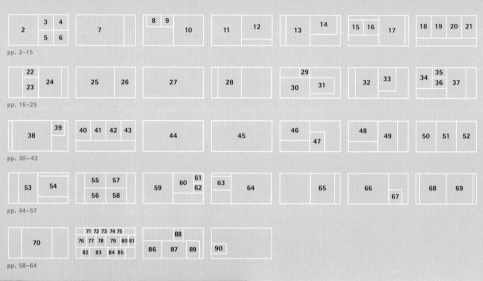

PHOTOS BY:

David Albanese:	11, 12, 13, 15, 16, 26, 27, 28, 34, 42, 43, 44, 60, 61, 62, 65, 66, 67, 69, 70, 74, 78, 85, 89
Cindy Anderson:	4, 31, 46, 55, 56, 57, 73
Bart Bartholomew:	20, 29, 30, 39, 50, 64
Edward Carreón:	90
Cherie Chen:	36, 53, 84
Claire Curran:	3, 5, 6, 23, 63, 76, 79, 81, 82, 83, 87
Alexander Vertikoff:	7, 8, 9, 14, 17, 19, 21, 22, 24, 35, 37, 38, 45, 47, 48, 49, 51, 54, 86, 88
Dominique Vorillion:	1 (cover), 2, 10, 18, 25, 32, 33, 40, 41, 52, 58, 59, 68, 71, 72, 75, 77, 80

DESIGN BY Markus Brilling
TEXT BY Jeffrey Hirsch
MANAGING EDITOR William Hackman
PHOTO EDITOR Kate Moodie
EDITOR Mollie Holtman
PRODUCTION COORDINATOR Suzanne Meilleur

© **1998 THE J. PAUL GETTY MUSEUM**
1200 Getty Center Drive
Suite 1000
Los Angeles, California 90049-1687

Library of Congress Card Number 98-42803
ISBN 0-89236-547-1